WILD *about* VENISON

Stoeger Publishing
Great Outdoor Books Since 1925

STOEGER PUBLISHING COMPANY
is a division of Benelli U.S.A.

Benelli U.S.A.
Vice President and General Manager: Stephen Otway
Director of Brand Marketing and Communications:
  Stephen McKelvain

Stoeger Publishing Company
President: Jeffrey Reh
Publisher: Jay Langston
Managing Editor: Harris J. Andrews
Design & Production Director: Cynthia T. Richardson
Photography Director: Alex Bowers
Imaging Specialist: William Graves
Copy Editor: Kate Baird
Editorial Assistant: Christine Lawton
Proofreader: Celia Beattie

Published by Stoeger Publishing Company
17603 Indian Head Highway, Suite 200
Accokeek, Maryland 20607

BK6476
ISBN: 0-88317-240-2
Library of Congress Control Number: 2002091616

Manufactured in the United States of America.

Distributed to the book trade and
to the sporting goods trade by:
Stoeger Industries
17603 Indian Head Highway, Suite 200
Accokeek, Maryland 20607

First of six in the *Wild About* cookbooks series.

Printed in Canada.

Contents

Introduction

While most commonly associated with the meat of the white-tailed deer, the word venison is a generic term that Webster's Dictionary defines as "an animal of the deer kind." Proper dressing and preparation of venison are of vital importance to its taste on the table. The carcass should be field-dressed immediately, with the remainder of the process taking place as soon as is feasible. Ideally, the meat should then hang or age for 7 to 10 days, at temperatures in the 36 to 40 degrees Fahrenheit (2.2 to 4.4 degrees Celsius) range, prior to butchering.

This book will help you discover exciting recipes that are at once delicious and easy to prepare. You will see how easy it is to use venison in a number of culinary contexts and that recipes calling for beef, veal or lamb can, in fact, use this meat as a substitute. What's more, most of the dishes offered here can be made using not only venison but also a variety of wild game.

Contrary to popular belief, wild meat doesn't necessarily have a "gamy" aftertaste. It all depends on the animal's eating habits; how the meat has been processed, aged and prepared; and especially the quantity of fat left on the meat. Fat is what gives venison a more pronounced taste, and it is best to remove as much of it as possible. The same holds true for sinew and silver skin. Since the meat of female deer and younger animals has a less pronounced taste and is tenderer, these meats are best cooked quickly over high heat, with the tenderest cuts served rare or medium-rare. Meat from older animals, particularly males killed during the rut, generally tastes better when marinated or cooked for longer periods over low heat. This is especially true for the tougher cuts.

Butcher cuts for wild game are quite similar to those for beef. The quantity of meat recovered will depend on a variety of factors, most notably shot placement. It is recommended that all the damaged flesh around bullet entry and exit points be discarded when dressing the animal. On the average, expect approximately 30 to 35 percent of the live weight of a caribou to be usable meat. This figure rises to 35 to 45 percent for white-tailed deer, mule deer and antelope, while for elk and moose 50 to 60 percent of the meat is suitable for the table. Ground meat helps reduce the quantity of tougher cuts (breast, front shank and neck), which require longer cooking times.

Most top chefs agree that the meat of wild game is the most savory of all meats. This results in part from its low-fat content and distinctive flavor. Better still, wild meat has a number of distinct health benefits. Low in cholesterol, venison is sometimes the only red meat individuals with heart problems

should eat. Similarly, wild game has never been tainted by the use of inoculants, growth hormones, and other approaches commonly employed in raising domestic animals. Instead, wild game enjoys a healthy, vegetarian diet, consuming foods that grow wild in their natural habitats. These animals eat according to their needs, and the fact that they are highly active accounts for their lower percentage of body fat and increased protein levels.

Of course, it is possible for wild game to consume some environmental contaminants, and keep in mind that the liver is a filtration system where the highest concentration of any pollutants will typically be found. One other vital health consideration focuses on the disease known as toxoplasmosis. It can be acquired through eating undercooked venison, and freezing the meat reduces the likelihood of infection but does not eliminate it. A woman who becomes infected with toxoplasmosis during pregnancy risks significant problems with the fetus she is carrying. These include death, brain damage, hydrocephalus, jaundice, or convulsions at or shortly after birth. To be perfectly safe, pregnant women should not eat or handle venison at all. If they do eat it, thorough cooking, with all the meat reaching temperature levels above 165 degrees Fahrenheit (74 degrees Celsius), is essential.

Otherwise, venison is a healthy, tasty meat, which can bring culinary delight. *Bon appétit*, and don't forget to ask your butcher to set aside the bones for making delicious stocks!

Fondue Stock

Method

1 POT

1. In a large pot, heat the oil and melt the butter. Cook the shallots, garlic and mushroom stems lightly, without browning them.

2. Moisten with the red wine and the stock. Bring to a boil and simmer for several minutes.

3. While cooking, add the flavorings (rosemary, thyme, bay leaf, peppercorns and salt). Remove them from the stock before final use.

4. Fill your fondue pot with the very hot stock before sitting down at the table so there will be enough stock for refills over the course of the meal.

5. Serve accompanied with thin slices or strips of venison and vegetables that you will cook in the stock at the table.

★ *Use the mushroom caps as a vegetable for cooking in the stock.*

Ingredients

1 tbsp	oil	15 ml
1 tbsp	butter	15 ml
3	shallots, chopped	3
3	cloves garlic, halved	3
12	mushroom stems*	12
1 cup	red wine	250 ml
8 cups	game stock (deer) or consommé	2 l
1	sprig of rosemary	1
2	sprigs of thyme	2
1	bay leaf	1
4 or 5	peppercorns	4 or 5
	salt to taste	

Variation

Oriental Stock: Replace the red wine with sake (rice wine). Replace the herbs with 1 tbsp (15 ml) of chopped fresh ginger, 2 or 3 sprigs of fresh coriander (or 10 to 12 coriander seeds) and 1 tsp (5 ml) of grilled sesame seeds.

Game Stock (Broth)

YIELD: 4 CUPS

Ingredients

2.2 lb	wild game bones	1 kg
3	carrots, cut into pieces	3
2	stalks celery, cut into pieces	2
2	onions, cut into pieces	2
1/4 cup	tomato paste	60 ml
2	cloves garlic	2
6 to 8	peppercorns	6 to 8
2	bay leaves	2
2	fresh sprigs of thyme **or**	2
1/2 tsp	dried thyme	2 ml
1	bunch of fresh parsley **or**	1
1 tsp	dried parsley	5 ml
6 cups	cold water	1.5 l

Method

1. Brown the meat and vegetables in a roasting pan in a 450°F (230°C) oven.
2. Add the tomato paste and continue cooking until roasted.
3. Transfer everything to a large pot, add the remaining ingredients, and bring to a boil.
4. Simmer uncovered for 3 hours.
5. Strain everything through a cheesecloth, and reserve the broth to make soups or sauces.

White-Tailed Deer

The white-tailed deer, also known as the Virginia deer, is the most common species of deer in North America. Forest clearing operations and wise game management practices have contributed to rapid growth of its numbers. Environments with dense forests hinder its ability to find suitable cover, and they also affect growth of the grasses, forbs and shrubs that figure prominently in the white-tail's diet. This species can be found near wooded areas, marshes, brush thickets and pastures or farm fields where there is cover nearby. Its fur is rust-color in summer and brownish gray in winter. The whitetail's main distinguishing characteristics are the white underside of its tail and the white or cream-colored stomach.

The white-tailed deer is between 4 and 6 feet long (1.2 and 1.8 meters) and has a shoulder height of between 2 ¾ and 3 ¼ feet (80 centimeters and 1 meter).

The males have multiple-tined antlers that shed in late winter each year, only to begin regrowing in the spring. Antler sizes vary according to the animal's eating habits and its age. A deer's age is calculated by measuring tooth wear. Deer tend to be primarily nocturnal in their movement patterns and are more easily spotted at dawn or dusk than during the middle of the day.

The white-tailed deer's diet is chiefly composed of twigs, buds and forbs in winter, complemented by grasses where available. In the more northern parts of its range the whitetail sometimes gathers in herds or deer yards in times of heavy snow. In warmer weather, major dietary sources include grasses, wild mushrooms and fruits, and in the fall whitetails feed heavily on both hard mast (acorns) and soft mast (apples, pears, wild grapes, persimmons and the like).

As with most deer species, the meat of the older animals and males in rut is less tender than that of females and younger animals, so you may want to marinate cuts from the former, or cook them using braising techniques. Many hunters prize the tongue and organ meats (brain, liver, heart and kidneys) of the whitetail, although it is generally agreed that the backstraps and tenderloins are the finest cuts.

Deer Liver in Savoy Cabbage Crown

4 SERVINGS

Ingredients

4	deer liver steaks	4
	milk for soaking	
	flour seasoned with salt and pepper	
1/4 cup	olive oil	60 ml
2	onions, sliced	2
2/3 cup	apple juice	160 ml
3	bacon slices, chopped	3
1	small Savoy cabbage, shredded	1
1	green apple, peeled and cubed	1

Method

1. If time permits, soak the liver in the milk overnight; otherwise soak for a minimum of 3 to 4 hours. Drain well.

2. Lightly flour the liver steaks.

3. Sear the meat in the olive oil in a well-heated skillet for 3 to 4 minutes on each side. Remove and keep warm.

4. Add the onions and cook over medium heat to soften them.

5. Deglaze with half of the apple juice and arrange the liver steaks on top of the onions to finish cooking, then set aside and keep warm.

6. Meanwhile, brown the bacon in a saucepan. Add the cabbage and the apple, cover and cook over medium heat for 4 to 5 minutes.

7. Add the remaining apple juice, season and slightly reduce.

8. Serve the liver with the onions, arranging in a crown of cabbage.

Barley and Venison Soup

Ingredients

1 tbsp	oil	**15 ml**
1	carrot, cut into pieces	**1**
1	stalk celery, finely chopped	**1**
1	onion, chopped	**1**
1/2 lb	deer meat, cut into strips or cubed	**225 g**
6 cups	game stock (deer)	**1.5 l**
1/2 cup	barley	**125 ml**
1	bay leaf	**1**
	pinch of dried thyme	
	salt and freshly ground pepper, to taste	

Method

1. In a large pot, heat the oil and sauté the vegetables.
2. Add the meat and sear it.
3. Moisten with the stock and bring to a boil.
4. Add the barley, bay leaf and thyme. Cook until the barley is tender.
5. Season to taste and serve the soup piping hot.

Oriental Sauté

4 SERVINGS

Ingredients

Marinade:

2/3 cup	plum sauce	**160 ml**
1/4 cup	concentrated orange juice	**60 ml**
1/4 cup	vinegar	**60 ml**
2 tsp	grilled sesame seeds	**8 ml**
1/2 tsp	salt	**2 ml**
1 1/2 lb	deer meat strips	**750 g**

Method

1. Mix the marinade ingredients together and set half the mixture aside.
2. Soak the deer strips in the marinade for a minimum of 30 minutes.
3. Arrange on skewers.
4. Cook the brochettes on a preheated grill.
5. Turn once, basting with the remaining marinade.

Venison Bourguignon

Ingredients

1 lb	deer meat, cubed	450 g
	sufficient quantity of flour	
1/4 cup	thin strips of lardons **or** bacon	60 ml
1 tbsp	oil	15 ml
2	cloves garlic, crushed	2
1/2 cup	small white pearl onions	125 ml
1 cup	white mushrooms, quartered	250 ml
1 cup	red wine	250 ml
1 1/2 cups	game stock (deer)	375 ml
	salt and freshly ground pepper, to taste	
2 tbsp	chopped fresh parsley	30 ml

Method

1. Dust the meat cubes with flour and set aside.
2. In a skillet, sauté the meat cubes and lardons in the oil. Reserve.
3. Using the same skillet, add the garlic, onions and the mushrooms. Continue cooking for 5 minutes over medium heat.
4. Deglaze with the wine and reduce by half.
5. Return the meat to the skillet and add the remaining ingredients, except the parsley. Bring to a boil and simmer for 40 to 45 minutes, until the meat cubes are tender.
6. Season, sprinkle with the parsley and serve immediately.

Wild Game Meat Pie

4 SERVINGS

Ingredients

8 oz	small cubes of deer meat	240 g
4 oz	small cubes of veal	100 g
4 oz	small cubes of pork	100 g
1	onion, chopped	1
1	clove garlic, crushed	1
1/3 cup	carrots, cut into small cubes	80 ml
1/4 cup	fennel bulb, cubed	60 ml
1/2 cup	yams, cut into small cubes	125 ml
1 cup	game stock (deer)	250 ml
	salt and freshly ground pepper, to taste	
1	layer of shortcrust pastry	1
1	egg, beaten	1

Method

1. Combine the meats, onion, garlic, carrots and fennel. Let stand a few hours in the refrigerator.

2. Preheat the oven to 350°F (175°C).

3. Place half the meat mixture in an ovenproof dish. Cover with a layer of potatoes, season and add the other half of the meat mixture.

4. Pour in the game stock, cover with the pastry crust, and cut several openings in the crust to allow evaporation.

5. Brush the crust with the egg and cook in the center of the oven for 1½ hours.

6. Serve immediately, accompanied with your favorite vegetables.

Sicilian Deer Stew
in Strong Beer

Ingredients

1 1/2 lb	deer meat cubes	675 g
2	shallots, minced	2
1 tbsp + 1 tsp	vegetable oil	15 ml + 5 ml
	salt and freshly ground pepper, to taste	
1 1/2 cups	game stock (deer)	375 ml
1 bottle (1 1/3 cups)	strong beer	1 bottle (341 ml)
1 bunch (8 oz)	sliced mushrooms	1 bunch (227 g)
2	tomatoes, seeded and quartered	2
1 can (14 oz)	quartered artichoke hearts	1 can (398 ml)
2 tbsp	flour mixed in water	30 ml
1/4 cup	whipping cream	60 ml

Garnish:

	sliced black olives	
	shredded fresh sage leaves	

Method

1. In a skillet, sauté the meat cubes and the shallots in 1 tbsp (15 ml) oil. Season.
2. Deglaze with the stock and the beer, bring to a boil, and simmer for approximately 1½ hours.
3. Strain and reserve the stock.
4. In the same skillet, cook the mushrooms, tomatoes and artichoke hearts in the remaining 1 tsp (5 ml) oil for 2 minutes. Reserve.
5. Add the stock to the skillet, and bring to a boil. Add the flour and whisk to thicken.
6. Add the cream, return the meat cubes and vegetables to the sauce. Season to taste.
7. Serve garnished with black olives and sage leaves.

Country Burgers

Method

1. Mix all the ingredients together, except the cheese.
2. Shape into patties, placing a slice of cheese in the middle of each.
3. Cook on a preheated grill or in a skillet, and finish cooking in the oven at 350°F (175°C).
4. Serve as is or as a traditional burger, accompanied with Dijon mustard and homemade mayonnaise.

Ingredients

1 lb	ground deer meat	450 g
1	egg, beaten	1
1/2 cup	chopped onion	125 ml
2	cloves garlic, minced	2
1/4 cup	chopped fresh parsley	60 ml
	steak spices, to taste	
2 tbsp	breadcrumbs	30 ml
	salt and freshly ground pepper, to taste	
3 oz	Swiss cheese, thickly sliced	90 g

Venison Steak
in Blueberry Sauce

Ingredients

3 tbsp	butter	**45 ml**
4	deer steaks	**4**
2	shallots, chopped	**2**
3 tbsp	flour	**45 ml**
1/3 cup	red wine	**80 ml**
2 cups	game stock (deer)	**500 ml**
1/2 cup	blueberries, fresh or frozen and drained	**125 ml**
	fresh or dried thyme, to taste	
	salt and freshly ground pepper, to taste	

Method

1. In a saucepan, melt the butter to sear the venison. Transfer to an ovenproof dish and keep warm.
2. Gently cook the shallots in the saucepan, without browning them.
3. Dust with the flour. Continue cooking until the flour turns a brownish color.
4. Deglaze with the wine and reduce by half.
5. Add the stock, whisking constantly.
6. Bring to a boil, then simmer until desired consistency.
7. Add the blueberries and the thyme, then season to taste.
8. Serve this sauce with the venison and your favorite steamed vegetables.

Roast Deer Fillet with Nutmeg, Cinnamon and Ginger Glaze

Ingredients

Ground Spices:

1 tsp	nutmeg	5 ml
1 tsp	cinnamon	5 ml
1 tsp	ginger	5 ml
1	vanilla bean, scraped and halved	1
1 1/3 lb	deer fillet, quartered	600 g
1 tbsp	oil	15 ml

Sauce:

1/3 cup	white wine	80 ml
2/3 cup	whipping cream or heavy cream	160 ml
	salt and freshly ground pepper, to taste	

Method

1. Preheat the oven to 375°F (190°C).
2. On a plate, mix the spices together and roll the meat in this mixture to cover.
3. In a saucepan, brown the meat in the oil and transfer to an ovenproof dish. Cook in the center of the oven for approximately 10 minutes.
4. Meanwhile, return the saucepan to the heat. Deglaze with the white wine and reduce by a third.
5. Add the cream and simmer to desired consistency.
6. Season to taste.
7. Serve the venison sliced over the sauce.

Roast Venison with Watercress and Basil Cream Sauce

Ingredients

2 tbsp	butter	30 ml
1 1/3 lb	deer roast	600 g
1	onion, sliced	1
1	clove garlic, halved	1
2 cups	watercress, stems removed	500 ml
1/4 cup	basil, compacted	60 ml
	salt and freshly ground pepper, to taste	
1/2 cup	game stock (deer)	125 ml
1/4 cup	light cream	60 ml

Method

1. In an ovenproof saucepan, melt half of the butter and sear the roast on all sides. Finish cooking in a 375°F (190°C) oven for 15 to 20 minutes, or more for desired doneness. Let stand 5 minutes before carving.

2. Meanwhile, place the remaining butter in a skillet and gently cook the onion and the garlic without browning them.

3. Add the watercress and the basil, then cover to wilt the leaves. Season to taste.

4. Moisten with the stock and simmer for 7 to 8 minutes.

5. Shred in a food processor or mixer and add the cream. Adjust the seasoning as needed.

6. Serve the roast slices coated in the sauce, accompanied with duchess potatoes.

Deer Filet Mignon
in Grand Marnier Sauce

Ingredients

1 tbsp	oil	15 ml
4	deer filet mignons, 5 oz (150 g) each	4
3 tbsp	brandy	45 ml
3 tbsp	Grand Marnier	45 ml
2 tbsp	cider vinegar	30 ml
1 cup	game stock (deer)	250 ml
	salt and freshly ground pepper, to taste	

Method

1. Preheat the oven to 425°F (220°C).

2. In a saucepan, heat the oil and sear the venison. Transfer to an ovenproof dish.

3. Finish cooking in the oven for approximately 5 to 7 minutes.

4. Drain any excess fat from the saucepan and return to the heat.

5. Deglaze with the brandy, Grand Marnier and vinegar. Reduce by half.

6. Incorporate the stock and simmer until a light sauce is obtained. Season to taste.

7. Serve the filet mignons on the sauce, accompanied with your favorite garnish.

Venison Steaks, Forestière Sauce

4 SERVINGS

Ingredients

1 tbsp	oil	15 ml
1 tbsp	butter	15 ml
4	deer steaks	4

Sauce:

1	shallot, chopped	1
1	clove garlic, minced	1
2 tbsp	butter	30 ml
2 cups	sliced wild mushrooms	500 ml
1/2 tbsp	flour	7 ml
1/2 cup	white wine	125 ml
2 cups	game stock (deer)	500 ml
1/3 cup	whipping cream	80 ml
	herbes de Provence, to taste*	
	salt and freshly ground pepper, to taste	

* *Herbes de Provence is a mix of rosemary, sage, oregano, marjoram and savory, which originates from the south of France.*

Method

1. Preheat the oven to 350°F (175°C).

2. In a saucepan, heat the oil and melt the butter to sear the venison. Transfer to an ovenproof dish and continue cooking in the oven for 5 to 6 minutes, or to desired doneness.

3. In the same saucepan, gently cook the shallot and garlic in half the butter without browning them. Add the mushrooms and continue cooking for several minutes. Reserve.

4. Melt the remaining butter in the saucepan and add the flour.

5. Moisten with the wine and the stock, whisking constantly. Bring to a boil and simmer until thickened.

6. Add the cream and the herbs and seasoning. Add the cooked mushrooms.

7. Check the consistency, reducing longer if required, and season to taste.

8. Serve with the venison steaks.

Deer Cutlets in Cream Sauce

Ingredients

4	deer cutlets	4
	sufficient quantity of flour	
	salt and freshly ground pepper, to taste	
2 tbsp	butter	30 ml
1 tbsp	oil	15 ml
2 tbsp	finely chopped onion	30 ml
1/2 cup	white wine	125 ml
1 cup	whipping cream	250 ml
2 tbsp	fresh herbs of your choice	30 ml

Method

1. Dredge the cutlets in the flour and season to taste.

2. In a saucepan, sear the cutlets over high heat in the butter and oil. Set aside and keep warm.

3. Gently cook the onion in the same saucepan, without browning it. Deglaze with the white wine and reduce by half.

4. Add the cream and reduce the liquid by half or to desired consistency. Season and add the herbs.

5. Serve the cutlets coated with the sauce, accompanied with egg noodles and your favorite vegetables.

Venison Steaks
in Creamy Brie Sauce

Ingredients

4	deer steaks	4
1 tbsp	oil	15 ml
1 tbsp	butter	15 ml
1	shallot, minced	1
1 tbsp	flour	15 ml
1/2 cup	white wine	125 ml
1 1/2 cups	game stock (deer)	375 ml
1/3 cup	light or whipping cream	80 ml
4 1/2 oz	Brie, in chunks	130 g
	salt and freshly ground pepper, to taste	

Method

1. In a saucepan sear the steaks in the oil and butter over high heat. Set aside and keep warm.

2. In the same saucepan, gently cook the shallot without browning it.

3. Dust with the flour, then deglaze with the white wine.

4. Add the stock, whisking well, then simmer over medium heat for 5 to 6 minutes, until the sauce thickens.

5. Add the cream and cheese, melting over low heat. Season to taste.

6. Serve the steaks coated with the sauce.

Rack of Deer
in Mint-Flavored Maple Syrup

8 TO 10 SERVINGS

Ingredients

1/2 cup	maple syrup	125 ml
1/3 cup	Dijon mustard	80 ml
1 tbsp	chopped fresh mint	15 ml
1	clove garlic, minced	1
2.2 lb to 2.4 lb	short leg of deer	1 to 1.2 kg
	breadcrumbs	

Sauce:

1	shallot, chopped	1
1	clove garlic, minced	1
2 tsp	butter	10 ml
1/4 cup	white wine	60 ml
1 package	prepared demi-glace	1 package
1 1/3 cups		330 ml
1 to 2 tbsp	maple syrup	15 to 30 ml
1 tsp	mint	5 ml
	salt and freshly ground pepper, to taste	

Method

1. In a small bowl, mix together the maple syrup, Dijon, mint and garlic, then season to taste.

2. Brush this mixture over the leg of meat and dust with the breadcrumbs.

3. Sear in the oven at 450°F (230°C) for 10 minutes. Lower the heat to 350°F (175°C) to finish cooking (approximately 20 min./lb – 20 min./kg).

4. Cook the shallot and garlic gently in the butter, without browning them.

5. Deglaze with the white wine. Reduce by half.

6. Add the demi-glace and the syrup, and simmer for 5 to 6 minutes.

7. Add the mint at the last minute and adjust the seasoning.

8. Serve the leg sliced with the sauce.

Black-Currant Deer Chops and Caramelized Red Onions

4 SERVINGS

You can use other berries in this recipe: Blueberries, currants or cranberries add a delicious flavor to this dish.

Ingredients

Sauce:

1 cup	finely sliced red onions	**250 ml**
1 tbsp	oil	**15 ml**
2 tbsp	butter	**30 ml**
1/2 cup	white wine **or** cider	**125 ml**
1/2 cup	unsweetened black-currant jam	**125 ml**
	salt and freshly ground pepper, to taste	
4	deer chops, 5 oz (150 g) each	**4**

Method

1. In a skillet, caramelize the onions in the oil and butter over medium heat.
2. Deglaze with the wine or cider and reduce the liquid by half.
3. Add the jam and season to taste.
4. Continue cooking for 2 minutes.
5. Cook the chops on the grill and garnish with the glazed onions.

Loin of Deer with a Cider-and-Honey Glaze

4 SERVINGS

Ingredients

2	apples, finely sliced	2
1 tbsp	butter	15 ml
2	shallots, minced	2
1/4 cup	cider vinegar	60 ml
1/4 cup	honey	60 ml
1 tbsp	dried rosemary	15 ml
	salt and freshly ground pepper, to taste	
1 lb	deer loin	454 g
1 cup	game stock (deer)	250 ml
2 tsp (approximately)	cornstarch, mixed with water	10 ml (approximately)

Method

1. In a saucepan, lightly brown the apples in the butter.

2. Add the shallots and cook for 2 minutes.

3. Deglaze with the cider vinegar.

4. Add the honey and rosemary, bring to a boil, and simmer for several minutes.

5. Season this reduction. Baste the loin with this mixture before and during cooking.

6. Place on a very hot grill to sear the meat, then lower the heat to medium and continue cooking for 10 to 15 minutes.

7. Add the game stock to the remaining reduction juices and bring to a boil.

8. Whisk in the cornstarch to thicken this sauce. Adjust seasoning as required.

Venison Osso Buco

Ingredients

8	1-in. (2.5-cm)-thick slices of deer hind shank	8
2 tbsp	oil	30 ml
1 tbsp	butter	15 ml
1	large onion, chopped	1
3	carrots, finely sliced	3
3	stalks celery, cut into pieces	3
3	cloves garlic, crushed	3
1 cup	game stock (deer)	250 ml
1 can (28 oz)	diced Italian tomatoes	1 can (796 ml)
1 cup	white wine	250 ml
2	bay leaves	2
	salt and freshly ground pepper, to taste	
	zest of 1 lemon	
1/4 cup	chopped fresh parsley	60 ml

Method

1. In a skillet, brown the shank slices over high heat in the oil and butter. Reserve.
2. In the same skillet, gently cook the vegetables for 3 to 5 minutes over medium heat, without browning them.
3. Add the meat slices and the remaining ingredients, except the lemon zest and parsley.
4. Simmer over low heat until the meat is tender, approximately 45 minutes to 1 hour.
5. Season to taste and add the lemon zest and parsley.
6. Serve immediately, accompanied with a risotto.

Duo of Tongues Marengo-Style

Ingredients

1	fresh deer tongue	1
1	fresh veal tongue	1
1	onion, coarsely chopped	1
1	bay leaf	1
1 tbsp	oil	15 ml
1 cup	white pearl onions	250 ml
1 cup	quartered mushrooms	250 ml
2 cups	prepared demi-glace	500 ml
1 cup	cubed fresh tomatoes	250 ml
1/4 cup	chopped fresh parsley	60 ml
	salt and freshly ground pepper, to taste	

Method

1. In a saucepan, cover the tongues with cold water and bring to a boil with the onion and the bay leaf. Simmer for 1 hour over low heat.

2. Let the tongues cool in their cooking juice before peeling with a sharp paring knife. Cut the meat into fine slices and set aside.

3. In another saucepan, heat the oil and sauté the onions and mushrooms. Add the tongues and the demi-glace, and bring to a boil. Add the tomato cubes and parsley, and season to taste.

4. Serve the tongues on a bed of egg noodles.

Heart Sauté with Sweet Pepper Rainbow

Ingredients

1	deer heart	1
2 tbsp	oil **or** butter	30 ml
1	red onion, finely sliced	1
1/2	red pepper, cut into strips	1/2
1/2	orange pepper, cut into strips	1/2
1/2	yellow pepper, cut into strips	1/2
1/2	green pepper, cut into strips	1/2
1/2 cup	game stock (deer)	125 ml
	salt and freshly ground pepper, to taste	

Method

1. Trim and remove the nerves from the heart; slice.

2. In a saucepan, heat half the oil and sauté the onion and pepper strips. Remove and set aside.

3. In the same saucepan, heat the remaining oil and sear the heart slices to brown well.

4. Add the vegetables and the stock; season to taste.

5. Serve immediately, accompanied with your favorite garnish.

Mexican Stuffed Vegetables

Some vegetables, such as eggplant, require longer cooking times. Adjust cooking times to the vegetable chosen.

Ingredients

4	tomatoes **or**	4
2	eggplants **or**	2
4	peppers **or**	4
4	zucchini	4
1 tbsp	oil	15 ml
1 tbsp	butter	15 ml
1	onion, chopped	1
1	clove garlic, crushed	1
1	green pepper, diced	1
1	stalk celery, chopped	1
1	carrot, grated	1
1 lb	ground deer meat	450 g
1 cup	frozen niblet corn	250 ml
1 tsp	chili powder	5 ml
1 tsp	ground cumin	5 ml
1 tsp	ground coriander	5 ml
	hot pepper **or** hot sauce, to taste	
	salt and freshly ground pepper, to taste	
1 cup	grated Monterey Jack cheese	250 ml

Method

1. Hollow out the tomatoes, eggplants, peppers and zucchini, chopping up the flesh, and set aside.

2. Heat the oil in a large saucepan and melt the butter.

3. Sauté the remaining vegetables and the chopped vegetable flesh for 5 to 7 minutes.

4. Add the meat and continue cooking until the meat is thoroughly cooked.

5. During cooking, add the niblets and spices, and season to taste.

6. Stuff the vegetable shells with this meat mixture.

7. Cover with cheese and brown in a preheated 350°F (175°C) oven for 10 minutes or until cheese is browned.

8. Serve the stuffed vegetables with salsa, sour cream, guacamole and corn tortilla chips.

Deer Risotto

4 SERVINGS

Ingredients

2 tbsp	butter	30 ml
1/4 cup	oil	60 ml
1	onion, chopped	1
1	clove garlic, crushed	1
1 1/2 cups	Arborio rice	375 ml
2 cups	game stock (deer)	500 ml
1 cup	white wine	250 ml
1	bouquet garni*	1
2 tbsp	butter	30 ml
1 lb	deer meat, cut into strips	450 g
1	zucchini, finely sliced	1
1	red pepper, cut into strips	1
1 package (8 oz)	sliced mushrooms	1 package (225 g)
1/2 cup	freshly grated Parmesan cheese	125 ml
	salt and freshly ground pepper, to taste	

Method

1. In a large saucepan, melt the butter in the oil and gently cook the onion and the garlic, without browning them.

2. Add the rice and cook until it becomes translucent.

3. Add the stock and the wine, and bring to a boil.

4. Add the bouquet garni and cook covered over low heat for 16 to 18 minutes, stirring occasionally. Remove the bouquet garni at the end of cooking.

5. Meanwhile, melt the butter in a skillet and sauté the venison strips. Reserve.

6. In the same skillet, brown the vegetables and add the cooked risotto, and return the meat to the skillet.

7. Add the Parmesan cheese and season generously.

8. Serve in deep serving plates.

* *Bouquet garni : A mixture of aromatic herbs attached with string to a section of leek in a cheese-cloth or between two celery sticks. It includes fresh parsley, thyme sprigs, bay leaves and peppercorns.*

Venison Chops with Pesto

Ingredients

Venison Chops:

1 tbsp	oil	**15 ml**
1 tbsp	butter	**15 ml**
4	deer chops	**4**
	salt and freshly ground pepper, to taste	
1/2 cup	basil pesto	**125 ml**

Pesto:

2	cloves garlic	**2**
1/4 cup	pine nuts, roasted	**60 ml**
1 bunch	fresh basil, washed and dried	**1 bunch**
1/4 cup	grated Parmesan cheese	**60 ml**
1/2 cup	olive oil	**125 ml**
	salt and black pepper, to taste	

Method

Venison Chops

1. In a skillet, heat the oil and melt the butter.
2. Cook the chops 5 minutes on each side, turning only once.
3. Season to taste and add the pesto to coat the chops well.
4. Serve the venison chops accompanied with your favorite pasta.

Pesto

1. In a food processor, chop the garlic and the pine nuts.
2. Add the basil and chop finely.
3. Blend in the Parmesan and gradually add the oil, mixing well.
4. Season to taste.

Note: Keep the pesto, covered in oil, in the refrigerator or freezer.

Mule Deer

The mule deer is so named because of its large ears, reminiscent of those of a mule. It has a rust-colored coat in the summer that turns to gray in the winter. The top or tip of its tail is black, making it easily recognizable. The mule deer's antlers have branches that normally divide into two stems, and they tend to be wider and heavier than those of the whitetail.

This animal is found primarily in western North America. It inhabits forests, mountains, hillsides, wooded valleys and brushy desert regions. It measures between $4\frac{1}{2}$ and $6\frac{1}{2}$ feet (1.4 and 2 meters) in length and can reach a shoulder height of 3 to $3\frac{1}{4}$ feet (90 centimeters to 1 meter). In the winter, mule deer can be seen in small groups on the lower slopes of mountains. They return to higher ground with the coming of spring.

Mule Deer Sauté in Hoisin Sauce

Ingredients

2 tbsp	oil	30 ml
1	onion, sliced	1
2	cloves garlic, minced	2
1 1/3 lb	mule deer, cut into strips or sliced cutlets	600 g
2 tsp	chopped fresh ginger	10 ml
1/2 tsp	five-spice powder *	2 ml
1/2 cup	hoisin sauce	125 ml
1 to 2 tbsp	honey	15 to 30 ml
	chopped fresh coriander, to taste	

Method

1. Heat the oil in a wok over high heat and sauté the onion and garlic.

2. Add the venison and sear quickly (in 2 or 3 batches, if the wok is small).

3. Add the ginger and sprinkle with the spices; cook for 2 to 3 minutes.

4. Add the hoisin sauce and the honey, mixing well to coat the meat.

5. Sprinkle with the coriander just before serving. Accompany with rice and sautéed vegetables.

* You can make your own five-spice powder by blending equal amounts of ginger, fennel, cinnamon and anise. Add a dash of cloves.

Mule Deer Stuffed
with Mushroom Duxelles

Ingredients

4	mule deer cutlets, boned	4
1 lb	mushrooms, finely chopped	454 g
1/4 cup	white wine	60 ml
1/4 cup	35% whipping cream or 15% cream	60 ml
	salt and freshly ground pepper, to taste	

Sauce:

2 cups	chicken stock	500 ml
1 tbsp	cornstarch	15 ml
1/4 cup	white wine	60 ml
1/4 cup	35% whipping cream or 15% cream	60 ml

Method

1. Flatten out the cutlets using a butcher's hammer or a heavy saucepan.

2. Cook the mushrooms in a saucepan until all juices have evaporated.

3. Deglaze with the white wine, add the cream and season. Reduce until almost dry. Set aside this mixture (duxelles) to cool.

4. Stuff the cutlets with the duxelles mixture.

5. Roll up and wrap in plastic wrap. Twist the ends in opposite directions to seal the roll (or ballotine), then wrap in aluminum foil. (Once heated, the aluminum foil will keep the plastic from melting on the roll.)

6. Cook in a preheated 375°F (190°C) oven for 30 to 35 minutes.

Sauce

1. Bring the stock to a boil.

2. Mix the cornstarch with the wine, add to the hot stock, and whisk until thickened to desired consistency.

3. Season and add the cream just before serving.

Mule Deer Brochettes

4 SERVINGS

Ingredients

Marinade:

1 cup	oil	**250 ml**
2 tbsp	cider vinegar	**30 ml**
3 tbsp	soy sauce	**45 ml**
1/2 cup	chili sauce	**125 ml**
1/2 cup	ketchup	**125 ml**
1	onion, finely chopped	**1**
1	bay leaf	**1**
1/4 cup	chopped fresh coriander	**60 ml**
1/4 tsp	ground pepper	**1 ml**

1 lb	mule deer brochette cubes	**450 g**
8	cherry tomatoes	**8**
12	mushroom caps	**12**
1	green pepper, cut into 8 pieces	**1**
1	red onion, cut into 8 pieces	**1**

Method

1. Mix all the marinade ingredients together in a deep dish. Add the meat and marinate in the refrigerator for a minimum of 3 hours, mixing occasionally.

2. Drain the cubes and thread them onto skewers, alternating with the vegetable chunks.

3. Grill the brochettes for 5 to 6 minutes on each side on the barbecue, basting with the marinade several times during cooking.

4. Serve immediately, accompanied with French fries or rice and vegetables.

Apricot and Deer Curry

Ingredients

1	onion, chopped	1
3	cloves garlic, minced	3
2 tbsp	oil	30 ml
1 tbsp	butter	15 ml
1 lb	mule deer stewing cubes	450 g
1	green pepper, cubed	1
1 to 2 tbsp	curry paste, mild or hot	15 to 30 ml
2 tbsp	lime juice	30 ml
1 can (14 oz)	coconut milk	1 can (396 ml)
1 cup	dried apricots, quartered	250 ml
1/3 cup	dried raisins	80 ml
	salt, to taste	

Garnish:

chopped fresh mint **or** coriander

Method

1. Sauté the onion and garlic in the oil and butter.
2. Add the deer meat cubes and sear over high heat.
3. Add the green pepper and continue cooking for 3 minutes.
4. Incorporate the curry paste and stir well to properly coat the ingredients. Cook for another 2 minutes to increase the flavor of the spices.
5. Add the remaining ingredients and continue cooking for 1 hour over medium heat, until the meat is tender. Check the seasoning and quantity of curry paste.
6. Serve the curry over a bed of basmati rice, and sprinkle with fresh mint or coriander.

Mule Deer Sausages

6 SERVINGS

Ingredients

1 lb	ground mule deer meat	450 g
1/2 lb	ground pork	225 g
1	clove garlic, minced	1
1	egg, beaten	1
1/2 cup	breadcrumbs	125 ml
3/4 cup	water	180 ml
1 tbsp	chopped parsley	15 ml
	salt and freshly ground pepper, to taste	
2 tbsp	Dijon mustard	30 ml
2 tbsp	maple syrup	30 ml

Method

1. Mix all the ingredients together, except the mustard and syrup.
2. Shape into one large sausage or into smaller sausages.
3. Roll up in aluminum foil.
4. Cook in the oven at 350°F (175°C) for 25 minutes (less for the smaller sausages).
5. Mix the mustard and syrup together.
6. Remove the aluminum foil, and place the sausage on a grill.
7. Baste with the mustard mixture.
8. Return to the oven at 450°F (230°C) for approximately 15 minutes.
9. Baste and flip several times.
10. Serve hot or cold.

Fillet of Mule Deer
Stuffed with Goat Cheese Tapenade

4 SERVINGS

Ingredients

1	clove garlic	1
1/2 cup	pitted black olives	125 ml
4	sun-dried tomatoes, in oil, or rehydrated	4
3/4 cup	fresh unripened goat cheese	180 ml
4 portions of 1/3 lb each	mule deer fillet	4 portions of 150 g each
1 tbsp	oil	15 ml
1 tbsp	butter	15 ml
	salt and freshly ground pepper, to taste	

Method

1. Preheat the oven to 350°F (175°C).
2. Using a food processor, chop the garlic with the olives and dried tomatoes.
3. Add the cheese and mix well to obtain a smooth mixture. Season to taste.
4. Butterfly the meat, making a pocket in each piece.
5. Fill each fillet with a quarter of the stuffing, close over and secure with toothpicks or tie with kitchen string.
6. In an ovenproof saucepan, heat the oil and melt the butter.
7. Sear the meat in the very hot fat, season and finish cooking in the oven for approximately 20 minutes.
8. Serve the stuffed fillet whole or sliced.

Mule Deer Medallions in Cranberry Sauce

Ingredients

4	mule deer medallions, 5 oz (150 g) each	4
1 tbsp	oil	15 ml
1 tbsp	butter	15 ml
2	shallots, minced	2
1/3 cup	red wine	80 ml
1/2 cup	cranberry juice	125 ml
1 cup	fresh or frozen cranberries	250 ml
	salt and freshly ground pepper, to taste	
	sugar, to taste	

Method

1. In a saucepan, brown the medallions in the oil and butter for 2 minutes on each side. Remove and keep warm.

2. In the same saucepan, gently cook the shallots without browning them, deglaze with the red wine, and reduce by half.

3. Add the remaining ingredients and simmer until the cranberries are cooked. Season. Add sugar as required to offset the bitterness of the cranberries.

4. Serve the medallions over the sauce.

Dried-Tomato-Stuffed Chops

4 SERVINGS

Ingredients

12	dried tomato chunks	12
1 bunch (1/2 lb)	cooked spinach	1 bunch (227 g)
4 oz	groud meat, any	100 g
1	clove garlic, minced	1
1/2	onion, chopped	1/2
1/2 tsp	ground sage **or**	2 ml
1 tsp	chopped fresh sage	5 ml
	salt and freshly ground pepper, to taste	
4	mule deer chops, 4 oz (100 g) each	4

Method

1. Soak the tomatoes in hot water for approximately 10 minutes to soften them; drain.
2. Chop the tomatoes and spinach.
3. Mix the ground meat together with the tomatoes, spinach, garlic, onion, sage, and salt and pepper.
4. Cut open the chops lengthwise (butterfly).
5. Stuff the chops with the dried-tomato mixture.
6. Close with toothpicks.
7. Cook on a preheated medium-high grill for 10 to 15 minutes, turning only once.
8. Serve with grilled vegetables.

Caribou

Caribou inhabit the boreal forests, wetland and tundra of North America and are thus found almost exclusively in Canada. For much of the year their diet consists almost entirely of lichen and moss. In the winter, caribou will also eat twigs, and in the summer they diversify to include berries, mushrooms, forbs and even roots.

The caribou has a large frame, measuring between 6 and 8 feet (1.8 and 2.5 meters) in length, with a shoulder height of 3 ¼ to 4 feet (1 to 1.2 meters). Depending on whether it is a mountain, barren ground, or woodland caribou, the animal will weigh from 400 to 600 pounds (180 to 270 kilograms). This cervid's long legs enable it to gallop at speeds in excess of 35 miles (56 kilometers) per hour. The caribou's wide, flexible hooves function much like snowshoes in the winter and are perfect for walking in snow. In the summer, they enable the caribou to swim easily for long distances.

Unlike other cervids, the female caribou grows antlers, although her rack is not as large as that of the male. The caribou's distinctive rack boasts three tines, one of which forms a peak (or shovel) over its forehead. Its hindquarters and white neck also distinguish it.

Caribou travel in large herds, with the groups seemingly formed according to sex and age. The most nomadic of all the cervids, the animal's migratory patterns are governed by the seasons. Before migrating, groups of caribou gather in a large herd that can reach as many as 100,000 animals. Because they congregate this way, caribou make easy prey for hunters. What's more, they are not readily spooked, making it all the more easy for hunters to pick out trophy specimens from passing herds.

Caribou meat is one of the tastiest of all wild meats. Its meat is sublime, particularly the variety meats, which are most tasty indeed.

Baked Blue Cheese
and Pine Nut Caribou Sirloin

Ingredients

Crust:

1 or 2	cloves garlic, minced	1 or 2
4 1/2 oz	crumbled blue cheese	140 g
1/2 cup	regular or Italian breadcrumbs	125 ml
1/3 cup	chopped pine nuts	80 ml
1 tbsp	oil	15 ml
	salt and freshly ground pepper, to taste	
4	caribou sirloin steaks	4
1 tbsp	oil	15 ml
1 tbsp	butter	15 ml

Method

1. Preheat the oven to 450°F (230°C).

2. Mix together all the ingredients for the crust (add dried herbs if regular bread-crumbs are used).

3. In an ovenproof saucepan, sear the steaks in the oil and butter over high heat.

4. Spread the crust mixture over the steaks and cook in the oven for 5 to 10 minutes, until the crust is golden.

5. Serve immediately, accompanied with seasonal vegetables.

Caribou Paupiettes with Ground Cherries and Maple Nectar

4 SERVINGS

Ingredients

4	caribou cutlets, boned	4
Stuffing:		
1/2 lb	ground caribou meat	225 g
1/2 lb	ground lean pork	225 g
2	shallots, minced	2
1/2 cup	ground cherries (physalis)*, quartered	125 ml
1 tbsp	maple butter **or** maple syrup	15 ml
1 tbsp	chopped fresh herbs (savory, thyme, basil, etc.); if using dried herbs, use 1 tsp (5 ml)	15 ml
2 tbsp	vegetable oil	30 ml
1 tbsp	butter	15 ml
Sauce:		
3 tbsp	butter	45 ml
1	large shallot, minced	1
3 tbsp	flour	45 ml
1/2 cup	white wine	125 ml
2 cups	game stock (caribou)	500 ml
1/2 cup	ground cherries*, halved	125 ml
2 to 3 tbsp	maple syrup	30 to 45 ml
1 tbsp	chopped fresh herbs (same as for the stuffing)	15 ml
	salt and freshly ground pepper, to taste	

Method

1. Flatten the cutlets using a butcher's hammer or a heavy skillet.
2. Mix all the stuffing ingredients except the oil and butter together. Season.
3. Spread the stuffing on top of the cutlets. Roll up tightly and tie with kitchen string or secure with toothpicks.
4. In a large saucepan, heat the oil and melt the butter. Sear the paupiettes on all sides.
5. Remove and place in an ovenproof dish. Finish cooking in the oven at 375°F (190°C) for 15 to 20 minutes.
6. Meanwhile, melt the butter in the same saucepan and gently cook the shallot without browning it.
7. Dust with flour and cook for 2 to 3 minutes until the flour turns light brown.
8. Deglaze with the wine, incorporate the stock and whisk well. Bring to a boil and simmer until the sauce thickens to desired consistency.
9. Add the ground cherries, syrup, herbs and seasoning.
10. Coat the surface of a serving plate with the hot sauce and arrange the caribou paupiettes on top. Accompany with rice or barley and seasonal vegetables.

* *Ground cherries, also known as husk tomatoes, produce tiny tomato-like fruits in papery husks on low, lanky bushes.*

Moose

The moose is primarily found in Canada, the Rocky Mountains, and the New England states. Its preferred habitat is woodlands with water nearby. Some hunters use canoes on rivers or lakes to get close to the animals. It is said that the white man, not the American Indian, first introduced the moose call, which is used to mimic sounds of the animals during the rut.

Male moose have enormous, wide racks featuring numerous tines. These shed and regrow annually. The bull moose has a tuft of thick hair under its chin, with a hanging muzzle. The largest of all the cervids, the moose can grow to between 7 ½ and 10 feet (2.3 and 3 meters) in length and reach a shoulder height of 5 to 6 ½ feet (1.5 to 2 meters). Its weight can easily exceed 1,100 pounds (500 kilograms).

With the coming of autumn, the males fight in head-to-head combat for the right to mate with females. The moose is a good swimmer and can run with ease in the snow. It can also strike formidable blows with its hooves and antlers, making it a dangerous opponent.

The moose eats a minimum of 50 pounds (22 kilograms) of food daily. During the winter, its diet is composed of forest tree species such as fir, willow and maple. In the summer, it consumes leaves, grasses, moss and aquatic plants.

Sauté of Moose with Orange and Sesame Seeds

4 SERVINGS

Method

1. In a skillet, sauté the meat strips in the canola oil over high heat.
2. Add the sesame oil, ginger, garlic and hot peppers. Continue cooking for 1 minute.
3. Add the green onions, soy sauce, orange juice and zest, and spices. Bring to a boil.
4. Thicken the sauce to desired consistency with the cornstarch mixed in a little water.
5. Serve the sauté over a bed of rice noodles, accompanied with vegetables.
6. Sprinkle with sesame seeds.

Ingredients

1 lb	moose meat strips	450 g
2 tbsp	canola oil	30 ml
1 to 2 tbsp	grilled sesame seed oil	15 to 30 ml
1 tbsp	chopped fresh ginger	15 ml
2	cloves garlic, minced	2
2 or 3	whole dried hot peppers	2 or 3
1 bunch	green onions, sliced diagonally, **or** 1 onion, sliced	1 bunch
1/4 cup	soy sauce	60 ml
	zest and juice of 1 orange	
	pinch of five-spice powder	
	cornstarch as required	
	sesame seeds for garnish	

Marinated Herb-and-Garlic Brochettes

4 SERVINGS

Ingredients

Marinade:

3	cloves garlic, minced	3
2 or 3	sprigs of rosemary, chopped	2 or 3
2 tbsp	chopped fresh thyme	30 ml
2 tbsp	chopped fresh mint	30 ml
1/2 cup	olive oil	125 ml
	juice of 1 lemon	
	crushed or ground pepper, to taste	
1 1/2 lb	moose meat cubes	675 g

Method

1. Mix all the marinade ingredients together.
2. Skewer the moose meat cubes and soak in the marinade for at least 30 minutes (do not leave the brochettes in the marinade for more than 6 hours). Drain.
3. Cook over a very hot grill to desired doneness (moose meat is best cooked pink).
4. Serve with homemade tzatziki sauce, accompanied with pita bread and a Greek salad.

Tzatziki Sauce

(4 SERVINGS)

1 **cup**	plain yogurt (thick) **or** sour cream	250 ml
2	cloves garlic, crushed	2
1	greenhouse cucumber **or**	1
2	regular cucumbers, seeded and thinly sliced	2
	salt and freshly ground pepper, to taste	

1. Mix all the ingredients well.
2. Let stand at least 30 minutes before serving.

Moose Country Spread

1 PÂTÉ

Ingredients

8	bacon slices	8
1 lb	ground pork	454 g
1 lb	ground moose meat	454 g
1/2 lb	moose meat, cut into 1/4-in. (.6-cm) cubes	225 g
1	egg, beaten	1
1/3 cup	game stock (moose) or other	80 ml
1/3 cup	Madeira, sherry **or** brandy	80 ml
1/4 cup	chopped fresh parsley	60 ml
1 tbsp	lemon juice	15 ml
1 tbsp	lemon zest	15 ml
1/4 tsp	dried sage	1 ml
1/4 tsp	dried marjoram	1 ml
1/4 tsp	dried thyme	1 ml
1/4 tsp	ground pepper	1 ml
1/2 tsp	salt	2 ml

Method

1. Preheat the oven to 325°F (160°C).

2. Grease a cake pan measuring 9 in. by 5 in. (22.5 cm by 12.5 cm).

3. Line the pan with the bacon slices to cover the bottom and sides.

4. In a bowl, mix all the ingredients together to form a smooth mixture.

5. Spread the meat mixture into the pan, pressing down lightly. Cover with parchment paper or aluminum foil.

6. Place the pan on a rimmed baking sheet and cook in the center of the oven for 1½ hours. The baking sheet will collect any drippings that spill over.

7. Remove and cool for approximately 10 minutes. Drain any excess fat.

8. Place a weight (cans of tomatoes, for example) on top of the pâté to compress the meat. Chill fully in the pan, first at room temperature, then overnight in the refrigerator.

9. Unmold onto a serving plate, slice and serve accompanied with mustard, pickles and crusty bread or crackers.

Cocoa Moose

4 SERVINGS

Moose meat is best served pink.

Ingredients

1 1/2 lb	moose tenderloin	675 g
1/4 cup	chopped shallots	60 ml
2 tbsp	vegetable oil	30 ml
1/4 cup	wine vinegar	60 ml
2 tbsp	sugar	30 ml
1 cup	game stock (moose) **or** veal stock	250 ml
2 tbsp	cocoa powder	30 ml
	salt and freshly ground pepper, to taste	

Method

1. Preheat the oven to 400°F (200°C).

2. In an ovenproof saucepan, sear the meat over high heat, then finish cooking in the oven for 15 to 20 minutes.

3. Meanwhile, in a skillet, gently cook the shallots in the oil, without browning them.

4. Deglaze with the vinegar. Incorporate the sugar and reduce by half.

5. Add the stock and the cocoa, then continue cooking to desired consistency. Season to taste.

6. Let the meat stand for 5 minutes before slicing.

7. Serve covered with the sauce.

Roast Moose
in Horseradish Crust

6 SERVINGS

Ingredients

Crust:

1/3 cup	Dijon mustard	80 ml
1 to 2 tbsp	chopped horseradish	15 to 30 ml
2	cloves garlic, minced	2
1 tbsp	crushed peppercorns	15 ml
1/2 cup	breadcrumbs	125 ml
1	moose roast, approximately 2 lb (900 g)	1
1 tbsp	oil	15 ml
1 tbsp	butter	15 ml
	salt, to taste	
2 cups	game stock (moose)	500 ml

Method

1. Preheat the oven to 375°F (190°C).

2. Mix all the crust ingredients together and set aside.

3. In an ovenproof saucepan, sear the roast in the oil and butter mixture.

4. Pat the crust mixture on the roast to cover.

5. Cook in the oven for approximately 40 minutes for rare meat or according to desired doneness. Remove the roast from the saucepan and let stand for 5 to 10 minutes before slicing.

6. Meanwhile, return the saucepan to the heat and deglaze with the stock. Reduce by a third and serve with the sliced roast.

Moose Tournedos
with Green Peppercorn Sauce

Ingredients

4	moose tournedos	4
1 tbsp	oil	15 ml

Sauce:

1	shallot, minced	1
1 tbsp	butter	15 ml
1/3 cup	cognac **or** brandy	80 ml
1 cup	game stock (moose)	250 ml
2 tsp	butter	10 ml
2 tsp	flour	10 ml
	salt, to taste	
1 to 2 tbsp	fresh green peppercorns	15 to 30 ml
1/4 cup	35% whipping cream	60 ml

Method

1. Brush the tournedos with the oil and cook them on a preheated barbecue or in a 425°F (220°C) oven to sear them, and finish cooking at 350°F (175°C) (approximately 10 minutes or until desired doneness).

2. In a saucepan, cook the shallot in the butter.

3. Deglaze with the cognac, reducing by a third.

4. Add the stock and bring to a boil.

5. Mix the butter and flour together to obtain a pasty texture. Add this to the hot stock, whisking with a whisk. Simmer until the desired consistency is reached. Add the salt, green peppercorns and cream, then cook for several minutes.

6. Serve the tournedos coated with the green peppercorn sauce.

Wild Game Meat Loaf with Spinach and Ricotta

6 SERVINGS

Ingredients

1 1/2 lb	ground moose meat	675 g
1	onion, finely chopped	1
1/2 cup	breadcrumbs	125 ml
1	clove garlic, crushed	1
1 tbsp	tomato paste	15 ml
1	egg white, beaten	1

Stuffing:

1/2 cup	light ricotta cheese	125 ml
1 package (10 oz)	frozen chopped spinach	1 package (300 g)
	salt and freshly ground pepper, to taste	
1 can (10 oz)	cream of tomato soup	1 can (296 ml)

Method

1. Mix all the meat loaf ingredients together. Spread the meat mixture on a sheet of aluminum foil measuring 10 in. by 10 in. (25 cm by 25 cm) to obtain a square approximately 1 in. (2.5 cm) thick.

2. Mix all the stuffing ingredients together and spread out in the center of the meat mixture.

3. Roll up and seal the ends well.

4. Bake in the oven at 400°F (200°C) for 45 minutes.

5. Remove the aluminum foil and coat the surface of the meat loaf with the cream of tomato soup. Continue cooking for 25 minutes.

6. Let stand for 10 to 12 minutes before slicing and serving.

Hungarian Moose Fillet

4 TO 6 SERVINGS

Ingredients

1 1/2 lb	moose fillet	675 g
2 tsp	oil	10 ml
	salt and freshly ground pepper, to taste	
2 tsp	paprika	10 ml
2 sheets	phyllo pastry	2 sheets
2 tbsp	melted butter	30 ml
1/2 cup	spinach	125 ml
1	onion, chopped	1
1 or 2	cloves garlic, minced	1 or 2
1 cup	white wine	250 ml
1 1/2 cups	35% whipping cream	375 ml
1 tsp	paprika	5 ml
1 tbsp	chopped chives	15 ml

Method

1. Heat the fillet in the oil over high heat in an ovenproof saucepan.

2. Season the fillet with salt and pepper, and sprinkle it with the paprika.

3. Brush the phyllo pastry sheets with the melted butter and stack them on top of each other.

4. Cover the pastry with spinach.

5. Place the fillet in the center of the pastry and roll up, leaving the ends open.

6. Cook in a preheated 425°F (220°C) oven until the pastry is golden. Remove and keep warm.

7. Using the same saucepan, sauté the onion and garlic over medium heat.

8. Deglaze with the white wine, and reduce by a third.

9. Add the cream and paprika, and cook until the sauce thickens.

10. Incorporate the chives and season to taste.

Pronghorn Antelope

Its abdomen, hindquarters, two brownish—white neck stripes, a white rump patch and fawn-colored fur distinguish the pronghorn antelope. Its black horns, which shed and regrow annually, have curved tips and are forked. The antelope measures from 4 to 4.5 feet (1.2 to 1.4 meters) in length, with a shoulder height that ranges from 3 to 3 ¼ feet (90 centimeters to 1 meter).

The pronghorn antelope inhabits open plains and steppes. It is found from southern Saskatchewan through the western part of the United States to the plains of Mexico. The fastest animal in North America, this mammal can leap distances of 20 feet (6 meters), soon leaving its predators far behind.

Vegetable Roulade

Ingredients

1 tbsp	oil	15 ml
1 tbsp	butter	15 ml
1	clove garlic, crushed	1
1	onion, finely sliced	1
1	carrot, julienned	1
1	red pepper, finely sliced	1
1	yellow pepper, finely sliced	1
1	zucchini, julienned	1
	salt and freshly ground pepper to taste	
4	large antelope cutlets	4
1 cup	wild game stock (antelope)	250 ml
1 tsp	sugar	5 ml
1 tbsp	balsamic vinegar	15 ml

Method

1. In a skillet, heat the oil and melt the butter.
2. Gently cook the vegetables without browning them for 3 to 5 minutes, or until tender. Season to taste and set aside.
3. Flatten the cutlets using a butcher's hammer or the bottom of a heavy skillet.
4. Place a quarter of the vegetable mixture at one end of each cutlet. Roll up and secure with toothpicks or tie with kitchen string.
5. In the same skillet, sear the cutlets over high heat to cook. Remove and keep warm.
6. Meanwhile, add the remaining ingredients to the skillet and reduce the liquid by half or to desired consistency. Season to taste.
7. Serve the roulades sliced, coated with the sauce.

Bacon-Barded Antelope Tournedos with BBQ Sauce

Ingredients

Sauce:

1 tbsp	oil	15 ml
1	onion, chopped	1
1	carrot, grated	1
1	clove garlic, crushed	1
1 tbsp	minced fresh ginger	15 ml
1 cup	wild game stock (antelope)	250 ml
2 tbsp	brown sugar	30 ml
1 tbsp	vinegar	15 ml
1 tsp	mustard of your choice	5 ml
1 tsp	crushed chilies	5 ml
1 tsp	paprika	5 ml
2 tbsp	Worcestershire sauce	30 ml
1 tbsp	cornstarch, mixed with a bit of cold water	15 ml
	salt and freshly ground pepper, to taste	
4	antelope tournedos, barded with thick slices of bacon	4

Method

1. In a skillet, heat the oil and gently cook the onion, carrot, garlic and ginger, without browning them.

2. Deglaze with the game stock. Add the remaining ingredients, except the cornstarch. Bring to a boil and simmer for 10 minutes.

3. Thicken the sauce with the cornstarch mixture and season to taste. Cook until thickened, stirring, remove and keep warm.

4. Cook the tournedos on a hot grill to desired doneness.

5. Serve the tournedos coated with the sauce and accompanied with a fried vegetable julienne.

Bard (to): To tie fat around lean meats or fowl to keep them from drying out during roasting. The fat bastes the meat while it cooks (keeping it moist and adding flavor).

Elk

American Indians gave the name *wapiti* (white rump) to elk. This came from the fact that this animal's hindquarters are appreciably whiter than the rest of its coat, which is a rusty brown color. The elk grows to majestic proportions: 7 ½ to 9 ½ feet (2.3 to 2.9 meters) in length and 4 to 5 feet (1.2 to 1.5 meters) in shoulder height. The male carries an imposing rack of antlers, which it sheds and regrows annually.

As a result of uncontrolled hunting in the past, the elk became extinct over much of its original range in eastern North America, and only in the last decade have restocking efforts begun to see its return to some of its original range. Today, elk are found almost exclusively in the mountains, forests and valleys in the West, where they live in large numbers.

During the fall mating season, the males engage in combat—sometimes to the death—to establish breeding dominance. The males usually winter with their harems, but they leave them before the calving season. During the summer, females and their young remain in groups and males form bachelor herds.

Elk Confit

You can use less tender pieces for the confit, since the meat will become tender as it is cooked for several hours in the slow oven.

Ingredients

	sufficient quantity of coarse salt	
1 tbsp	sugar	15 ml
2 tbsp	cracked pepper	30 ml
2	bay leaves	2
1 tsp	dried thyme	5 ml
1	clove garlic, sliced	1
1/2 lb	elk meat pieces (cut in such a way as to retain the longest fibers)	225 g
	sufficient quantity of duck **or** goose fat (to cover the meat pieces)	

Method

1. Mix together the salt, sugar, pepper, bay leaves, thyme and the garlic.

2. Cover the game pieces with this salt mixture and marinate for 1 to 1½ hours.

3. Rinse the meat pieces in cold running water to remove all the salt.

4. Dry between absorbent paper towels to remove as much moisture as possible.

5. In an ovenproof saucepan, melt the fat, add the elk chunks, cover and cook in the oven at 200°F (100°C) for 3 to 6 hours, until the meat is tender.

6. Separate the elk confit and serve warm on a bed of spinach with your favorite vinaigrette.

Warm Elk and Nut Garden Salad

4 SERVINGS

Ingredients

	variety of mixed lettuce leaves	
2	carrots, sliced	2
1	apple, julienned	1
1 or 2	stalks celery, sliced	1 or 2
1/2	yellow pepper, julienned	1/2
2 tbsp	oil	30 ml
1 tbsp	butter	15 ml
1 lb	elk meat strips or small cubes	450 g
1	clove garlic, minced	1
1	shallot, chopped	1
3 tbsp	cider vinegar	45 ml
1 tbsp	Dijon mustard	15 ml
2 to 3 tbsp	maple syrup	30 to 45 ml
	salt and freshly ground pepper, to taste	
1/4 cup	dried cranberries (or other dried fruit)	60 ml
1/4 cup	crushed nuts	60 ml

Method

1. Combine the lettuce leaves, carrots, apple, celery and pepper. Arrange into a lettuce nest on each plate.

2. In a large saucepan, heat the oil and melt the butter. Sauté the meat with the garlic and the shallot.

3. Deglaze with the vinegar and add the mustard mixed with the maple syrup. Season to taste. Distribute on top of the lettuce nests.

4. Sprinkle each plate with the cranberries and nuts. Use the cooking liquid as a vinaigrette, serving immediately.

Simmered Elk and Roasted Garlic

Ingredients

2	heads of garlic	2
1 tbsp	oil	15 ml
1 tbsp	butter	15 ml
1 1/2 lb	elk meat stewing cubes	675 g
1	onion, coarsely chopped	1
1/4 cup	all-purpose flour	60 ml
4 cups	game stock (elk)	1 l
1	bouquet garni*	1
1 cup	carrot, cut into pieces	250 ml
2	stalks celery, cut into pieces	2
8	baby potatoes, quartered	8
	salt and freshly ground pepper, to taste	

Method

1. Peel the heads of garlic, cut the cloves in half, and remove the germ. In a skillet, roast the cloves in the oil and butter over low heat until they are golden and tender. Reserve.

2. Brown the meat cubes in the same skillet.

3. Add the onion and continue cooking for 2 minutes.

4. Dust with the flour, moisten with the stock and add the bouquet garni.

5. Bring to a boil and simmer for 1 hour.

6. Add the vegetables and continue cooking for 20 minutes.

7. Add the reserved garlic cloves and mix well.

8. Season to taste and serve in deep dishes, accompanied with chunks of toasted crusty bread.

* *Bouquet garni: A mixture of aromatic herbs attached with string to a section of leek in a cheese-cloth or between two celery sticks. It includes fresh parsley, thyme sprigs, bay leaves and peppercorns.*

Elk Cassoulet

Ingredients

3 1/2 cups	white **or** kidney beans	875 ml
1 lb	elk meat cubes, shoulder cut	450 g
4	thick slices of bacon, chopped	4
1	pork or wild boar hock, halved	1
2	onions, chopped	2
3	stalks celery, cut into pieces	3
3	carrots, cut into pieces	3
1	bay leaf	1
	pinch of dried thyme	
	sufficient quantity of water or game stock (elk)	
1/2 cup	maple syrup	125 ml
	salt and freshly ground pepper, to taste	

Method

1. In a large pot, cover the beans with cold water and bring to a boil. Simmer for 10 minutes, remove from heat, and cool in the water.

2. Drain, rinse and set aside.

3. In a heavy saucepan, brown the elk meat cubes with the bacon over high heat. Reserve.

4. In the same saucepan, brown the hock halves over high heat.

5. Add the elk meat cubes, beans, vegetables, bay leaf and thyme.

6. Cover with water. Cover the saucepan and bring to a boil, then simmer over low heat for 1½ to 2 hours, until the beans are tender.

7. Remove the hock; bone and remove the fat. Discard the bone, skin and fat, reserving only the meat. Return to the saucepan.

8. Add the syrup and season to taste. Serve immediately.

Wild Game Kebabs

Ingredients

1 1/2 lb	ground elk meat	675 g
1	egg, beaten	1
1	onion, chopped	1
2	cloves garlic, minced	2
1 tsp	cumin	5 ml
1/2 cup	breadcrumbs	125 ml
1/4 cup	ground pine nuts	60 ml
	salt and freshly ground pepper, to taste	

Method

1. Mix all the ingredients together. Divide the mixture into 6 portions.
2. Shape the mixture onto the brochette skewers.
3. Cook on the grill or in the oven at 375°F (190°C) for 20 to 25 minutes.
4. Serve with a yogurt sauce, accompanied with tabbouleh.

Grilled Elk
and Sweet Pepper Coulis

4 SERVINGS

I n g r e d i e n t s

4	elk steaks, 5 oz (150 g) each	4
1 tbsp	oil **or** butter	15 ml
1/2	onion, sliced	1/2
1	clove garlic, crushed	1
2	sweet peppers of your choice (yellow, orange, red), halved and seeded	2
1 cup	game stock (elk)	250 ml
1 tsp	fresh thyme	5 ml
1/4 cup	cream of your choice	60 ml
	salt and freshly ground pepper, to taste	

M e t h o d

1. Cook the steaks on the grill to desired doneness.

2. Meanwhile, in a skillet, sauté the onion and the garlic in the oil or butter.

3. Add the peppers and continue cooking for 2 to 3 minutes, covered.

4. Moisten with the stock, cover and cook for 10 to 15 minutes, until the peppers are tender.

5. Remove from heat and purée the peppers. Add the thyme, cream and season to taste.

6. Serve the steaks accompanied with the pepper coulis and your favorite seasonal vegetables.

Elk Whiskey Steak Flambé

Keep a skillet cover handy in order to extinguish any unruly flames resulting from the flambé process.

Method

1. In a skillet, sear the steaks in the oil and butter over high heat to desired doneness.

2. Add the whiskey and flambé. Let the flames extinguish themselves.

3. Add the cream and season to taste.

4. Serve the steaks accompanied with the sauce and sprinkled with parsley.

5. Accompany with a starchy food and seasonal vegetables.

Ingredients

4	elk steaks, 5 oz (150 g) each	4
1 tbsp	oil	15 ml
2 tbsp	butter	30 ml
1/2 cup	whiskey	125 ml
1/4 cup	35% whipping cream	60 ml
	salt and freshly ground pepper, to taste	
2 tbsp	chopped fresh parsley	30 ml

Elk Roll with Pears

4 SERVINGS

Ingredients

1 tbsp	butter	15 ml
2	cloves garlic, minced	2
2	shallots, minced	2
3	pears, peeled and cubed	3
1/2 tsp	ground nutmeg	2 ml
	salt and freshly ground pepper, to taste	
4	elk cutlets	4

Sauce:

1 tbsp	oil	15 ml
2 tbsp	butter	30 ml
1 1/2 tbsp	flour	20 ml
2/3 cup	dry white wine	160 ml
1 1/4 cups	game stock (elk)	310 ml

Method

1. In a large saucepan, melt the butter over high heat and cook the garlic and shallots gently, without browning them. Add the pear cubes and cook for several minutes, until tender.

2. While cooking, add the nutmeg and season to taste. The pear cubes must remain firm without becoming a purée.

3. Flatten the cutlets and place a quarter of the stuffing inside each cutlet. Shape into a cylinder with the stuffing at one end. Roll the cutlet up to cover the stuffing. Attach with toothpicks or tie with kitchen string.

4. In the same saucepan, heat the oil and melt the butter, then sear the stuffed cutlets on all sides and place them in an ovenproof dish. Finish cooking in a preheated 375°F (190°C) oven for at least 15 minutes, depending on the size of the cutlets.

5. Add the flour to the fat remaining in the saucepan to make a roux. Return to the heat and cook slowly while stirring continuously to obtain a light brown roux.

6. Deglaze with the white wine and reduce by a third. Moisten with the stock while stirring continuously. Bring to a boil and simmer until thickened.

7. Slice the elk rolls and arrange decoratively over the sauce. Garnish with small raw pear cubes, accompanied with your favorite seasonal vegetables.

Grilled Dijon
Elk Filet Mignon

Ingredients

Marinade:

1 tbsp	Dijon mustard	15 ml
1/4 cup	canola oil	60 ml
3 tbsp	red wine	45 ml
1/2	onion, sliced	1/2
1	clove garlic, minced	1
	ground pepper, to taste	
2	elk filet mignons, 5 oz (150 g) each	2

Sauce:

1	shallot, chopped	1
1 tsp	butter	5 ml
1 tbsp	flour	15 ml
1/4 cup	red wine	60 ml
1/2 cup	game stock (elk)	125 ml
2 to 3 tbsp	Dijon mustard	30 to 45 ml
	salt and freshly ground pepper, to taste	

Method

1. Mix all the marinade ingredients together and pour over the elk filet mignons in a dish to be marinated in for 1 to 2 hours.

2. Cook the meat on an oiled, preheated 375°F (190°C) grill. Season to taste.

3. Meanwhile, in a skillet, cook the shallot in the butter for 2 to 3 minutes.

4. Dust the shallot with the flour, mix well, and cook for another minute.

5. Deglaze with the wine, incorporate the stock and bring to a boil.

6. Add the mustard just before the end of cooking. Season with salt and pepper.

7. Serve the filet mignons accompanied with the sauce.

Tender Stuffed Chops

Method

1. Butterfly the chops.
2. Mix all the apple stuffing ingredients together in a bowl, then stuff the chops with this mixture.
3. Arrange the chops in a 12 in. by 8 in. by 2 in. (31 cm by 21 cm by 5 cm) microwaveable dish, meat side out, and set aside.
4. In a bowl, mix together the sweet glaze ingredients; brush the chops with half of this glaze mixture.
5. Cover the dish with wax paper, and cook on medium heat in the microwave for 35 to 40 minutes. After 15 minutes cooking time, rotate the dish half a turn.
6. Remove the chops from the oven and let stand for 5 minutes, basting with the remaining sweet glaze.
7. Serve accompanied with your favorite seasonal vegetables.

Ingredients

4	elk chops, 1 in. (2.5 cm) thick	4

Apple Stuffing:

2 cups	peeled and chopped apples	500 ml
1/4 cup	dried raisins	60 ml
1	egg, beaten	1
2 tbsp	melted butter	30 ml
1/2 tsp	cinnamon	2 ml
1/2 tsp	salt	2 ml
1/8 tsp	pepper	0.5 ml

Sweet Glaze:

1/3 cup	gooseberries	80 ml
2 tbsp	orange juice	30 ml

Tonkinese Soup
with Wild Meat

Method

1. Heat the oil in a saucepan and cook the onion, garlic and ginger gently, without browning them.

2. Moisten with the stock. Add the coriander stems (set aside the leaves for garnish) and the five-spice powder. Season to taste.

3. Strain the stock and keep hot.

4. Divide the noodles into four bowls, cover with the raw meat and the minced green onions.

5. Pour the boiling-hot stock over the meat to fill the bowls. The stock must be boiling in order to cook the meat.

6. Garnish and serve immediately so that each guest can season to their individual taste. Some people, for example, like to add crushed chili paste.

Ingredients

1 tbsp	oil	15 ml
1	onion, finely sliced	1
1	clove garlic, germ removed	1
1	chunk of ginger root	1
(1 in. sq.)		(2.5 cm. sq.)
8 cups	game stock (elk)	2 l
1/2 bunch	fresh coriander	1/2 bunch
	pinch of five-spice powder	
	salt and freshly ground pepper, to taste	
1 package (8 oz)	rice noodles, cooked	1 package (225 g)
1 lb	raw elk meat, sliced very thin (fondue meat)	450 g
1 bunch	green onions, minced	1 bunch

Garnish:

1	lime, quartered	1
2 cups	bean sprouts	500 ml
	fresh basil, to taste	
	coriander leaves	

Index